D1627868

WHY DO I

BLEED?

BY KIRSTY HOLMES

THE SECRET BOOK COMPANY

All rights reserved.
Printed in Malaysia.

A catalogue record for this book is available from the British Library.

ISBN: 978-1-78998-043-1

©2019
The Secret Book Company
King's Lynn
Norfolk PE30 4LS

Written by:
Kirsty Holmes

Edited by:
Madeline Tyler

Designed by:
Danielle Rippengill

All facts, statistics, web addresses and URLs in this book were verified as valid and accurate at time of writing.
No responsibility for any changes to external websites or references can be accepted by either the author or publisher.

WHY DO I BLEED?

IMAGE CREDITS

All images are courtesy of Shutterstock.com, unless otherwise specified. With thanks to Getty Images, Thinkstock Photo and iStockphoto.
Front Cover & 1 – Dmitry Natashin, Nadzin, Jemastock, hvostik. Images used on every spread – Nadzin, TheFarAwayKingdom. 2 – johavel,
anpanna4 – emastock, hvostik. 5 – Iconic Bestiary. 6 & 7 – johavel, anpannan, VasutinSergey. 8 & 9 – Andy Frith. 10 & 11 – LOVE YOU,
VasutinSergey. 12 & 13 – Creative Mood. 14 & 15 – vladwel, Elena Paletskaya. 16 – DRogatnev, Nadia Buravleva. 17 – svtdesign. 18 – naulicreative,
johavel, anpannan. 19 – gritsalak karalak. 20 – Photoroyalty. 21 – Lexamer. 22 – vladwel, Nadya_Ar. 23 – johavel, anpannan, wectors.

CONTENTS

Words that look like **this** can be found in the glossary on page 24.

DO YOU NEED A PLASTER?

Have you ever cut your finger, had a nosebleed or needed a plaster for your knee?

What is that red stuff that's everywhere, and what does it do?

When you break or cut your skin, that red stuff is your blood. Blood is very important – and it's supposed to stay inside you!

But what is it – and where does it come from?

WHAT IS BLOOD FOR?

All **mammals**, and most animals, are full of blood. We need it to live, and it has lots of really important jobs to do.

JOLLY GOOD STUFF

Blood helps carry important things, such as **<u>oxygen</u>**, around the body to where it's needed. It also helps to protect us from illnesses and heals our cuts and scrapes. But how?

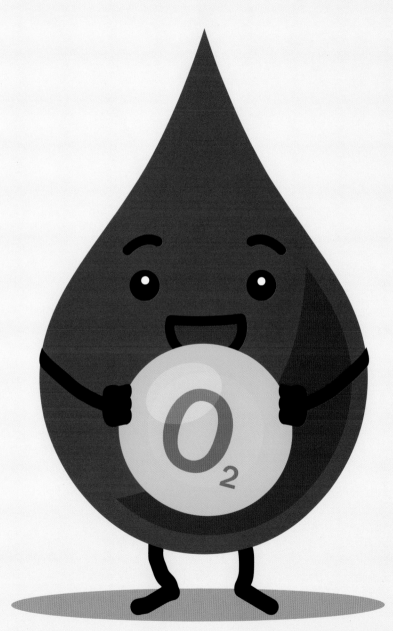

RED... OR WHITE?

What's in your blood?

Red blood cells carry oxygen around the body.

White blood cells attack and destroy diseases and germs.

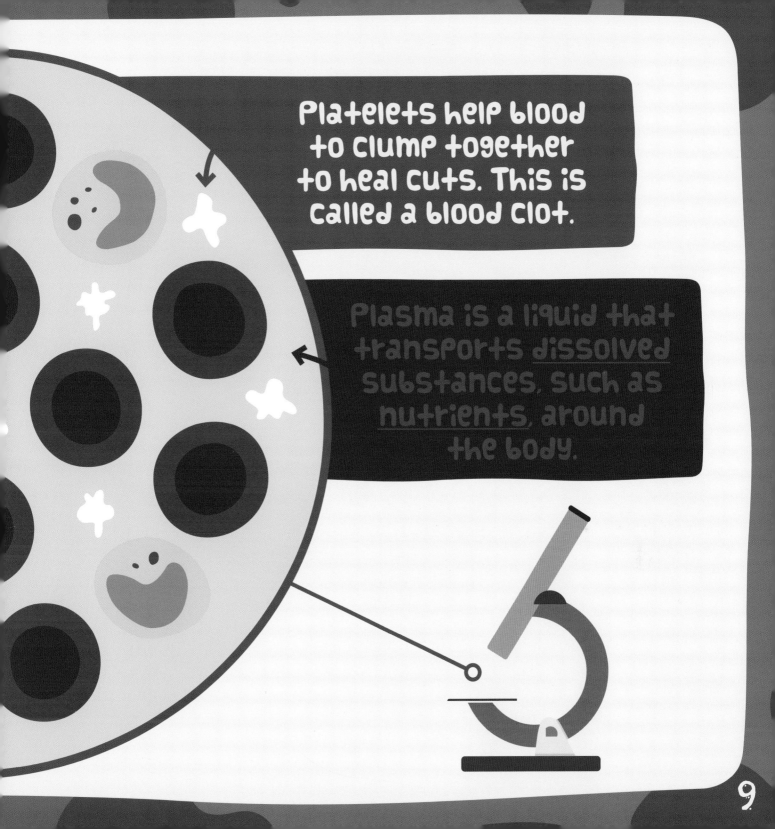

Platelets help blood to clump together to heal cuts. This is called a blood clot.

Plasma is a liquid that transports dissolved substances, such as nutrients, around the body.

LET'S GET AROUND

The circulatory **(SAY: SER-CU-LAY-TOR-EE)** system is very important.

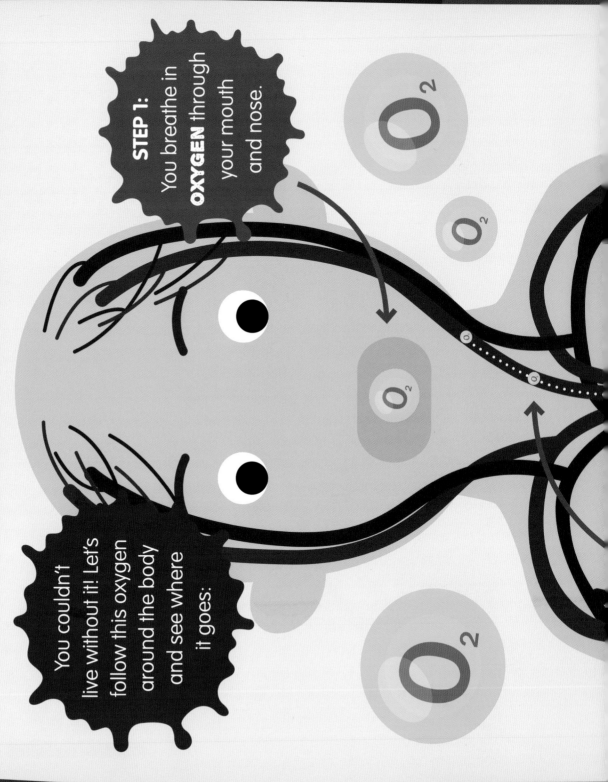

STEP 1: You breathe in **OXYGEN** through your mouth and nose.

You couldn't live without it! Let's follow this oxygen around the body and see where it goes:

STEP 3:
Your **HEART** beats like a pump, squeezing the blood around the body.

STEP 2:
Your **ARTERIES** carry blood filled with oxygen around the body.

STEP 4:
Your **VEINS** carry used blood back to the heart to be filled with oxygen from the lungs again.

PARTS OF THE HEART

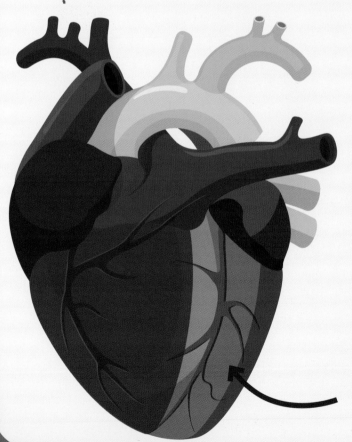

Your heart is a clever **organ**. It works like a pump to squirt your blood around your body.

Hold this book against your chest to see where it all goes!

The main chambers of the heart, on your left, are called the left ventricle. They send new blood, full of oxygen from the lungs, to the body.

The right ventricle takes the old blood from the body and sends it back to the lungs to be filled with oxygen again.

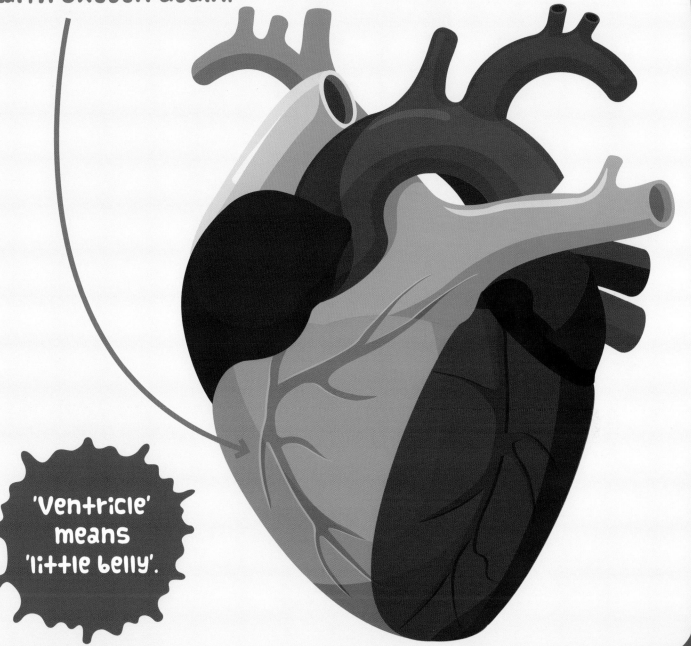

'Ventricle' means 'little belly'.

VEINS & ARTERIES

The tubes that take the blood from the heart around the body are called blood vessels, and there are two types.

Veins carry old blood back to the heart.

Arteries carry blood with oxygen from the left ventricle.

If you make a fist, squeeze tight and look at your wrist, you should be able to see your veins and arteries at work! Eww!

FEEL THE BEAT

As your heart pumps the blood around your body, it beats in a steady rhythm. If you listen to someone's chest, you will hear a bump-bump-bump sound. This is called a heartbeat.

BUMP
BUMP

BUMP
BUMP

A heart will beat over 2.5 billion times in an average lifetime!

SCABS & SCRATCHES

If you cut yourself by accident, or have a nosebleed, your blood will appear where it doesn't belong – on the outside!

RED ALERT!

RED ALERT!

Human beings recognise the colour red as meaning 'something's wrong'.

Your platelets spring to work, filling up the cut and stopping the bleeding. They make a hard, crusty top, called a scab, to stop the bleeding.

Never pick a scab - even if it's tempting. Let it fall off when it has done its job.

KNOW YOUR TYPE

A   B   AB   O

We all have a 'blood type'. This means blood comes in different kinds, based on what kind of red blood cells you have.

Sometimes, if someone loses a lot of their blood, we can give them more from a blood **donor**.

It's important to give someone the right type of blood.

Do you know your blood type?

BLOOD BUSTERS!

If you laid out all your blood vessels in a line, they would be around 100,000 kilometres long!

A whale's heart is so huge, it only beats around five times in a minute!

The pygmy shrew has the smallest heart of any mammal: as small as a thumbnail!

It only takes around 20 seconds for your blood to go all the way round your body!

GLOSSARY

cells	the basic units that make up all living things
dissolved	mixed completely with liquid
donor	a person who donates their healthy blood, organs or stem cells to help others
mammals	animals that have warm blood, a backbone and produce milk
nutrients	natural things that people need to grow and stay healthy
organ	a part inside a living thing that has a specific, important function
oxygen	a natural gas that all living things need in order to survive

INDEX